AYRSHIRE'S LAST DAYS OF ST

by
W.A.C. Smith

A cheery wave from the driver of a class 2P 4-4-0, no. 40610, as the 6.43 p.m. to Kilmarnock starts away from Ayr on the beautifully sunny evening of 18 June 1955. These Derby-built locomotives monopolised Ayrshire services for some thirty years, having replaced many former G&SW locomotives during the early years of the LMS.

© W.A.C. Smith, 2001
First published in the United Kingdom, 2001,
by Stenlake Publishing Ltd.
54–58 Mill Square,
Catrine, Ayrshire KA5 6RD
Telephone: 01290 551122
www.stenlake.co.uk

ISBN 1 84033 151 8

All photographs by W.A.C. Smith

The publishers regret that they cannot supply
copies of any pictures featured in this book.

A class 2P 4-4-0, no. 40592, awaiting departure from Darvel with the 7.05 p.m. train to Glasgow (St Enoch) on 16 May 1953. The towns of Galston and Newmilns in the Irvine Valley had been reached from Hurlford in 1850, but it was not until 1896 that a single track extension was made by the G&SW to Darvel. The Strathaven & Darvel Railway opened in 1905, being worked alternately by the G&SW and Caledonian, but was abandoned in 1939. The Darvel branch followed suit in 1964.

INTRODUCTION

The Glasgow & South Western Railway Company, more familiarly known as the Sou'West, was synonymous with Ayrshire and was formed on 1 October 1850 by the amalgamation of the Glasgow, Paisley, Kilmarnock & Ayr Railway and the Glasgow, Dumfries & Carlisle Railway. The railway age had, however, already arrived in Ayrshire in the form of the horse worked waggonways moving coal from pits to waterways and of these the Kilmarnock & Troon, promoted by the Duke of Portland, was the first railway in Scotland for which an Act of Parliament was obtained (in 1808) and also the first in Scotland (c.1817) to use a steam locomotive. In its final form the G&SW railway resembled a giant triangle with its apex at Glasgow, its sides utilising the Nith and Garnock valleys – the former reaching Dumfries and the latter route connecting with the Ardrossan Railway and extending south through Ayr to Stranraer – and its base formed by the line from Gretna to Portpatrick.

Curiously, access to Glasgow was over lines shared with the rival Caledonian Railway, namely the Glasgow & Paisley and Glasgow, Barrhead & Kilmarnock Railways, while Carlisle was reached by means of running powers over the Caledonian Railway from Gretna Junction. The 'Port Road' between Castle Douglas and Portpatrick was jointly owned by the G&SW, Caledonian, Midland and London & North Western Railways. Central Ayrshire was criss-crossed by G&SW mineral lines opened in the 1870s, some with meagre passenger facilities, but a potentially useful short cut which failed to materialise was from Kilmacolm, on the Greenock & Ayrshire Railway, to Largs.

In 1923, under the government inspired railway grouping of that year, the Sou'West became part of the London, Midland & Scottish Railway along with the Caledonian Railway and Highland Railway. Further reorganisation followed the railways' nationalisation in 1948 when the LMS lines in Scotland were merged with those of the London & North Eastern Railway (which until 1923 had been the North British and Great North of Scotland Railways) to form the Scottish Region of British Railways, now privatised as Scotrail.

The government funded Modernisation Plan of 1955 brought gradual dieselisation and the Beeching Plan of 1963 saw the closure not only of branch lines, but also of what were termed 'unremunerative' main lines which

The former Caledonian Railway 0-4-4T, no. 55203, awaits departure at Beith (Town) Station with the 7.30 p.m. to Lugton on 8 May 1954. Latterly operated by a diesel railbus, the eight mile branch from Lugton to Beith lost its passenger service in 1962. The 'Town' suffix had been added to distinguish the branch terminal from Beith (North) Station on the Kilwinning line.

included the one from Dumfries to Stranraer. This resulted in diversion of the Euston sleeper from Stranraer to Ayr with steam haulage until Ayr Motive Power Depot was closed to steam on 3 October 1966 (the service continued with diesel haulage). The last Scottish Region steam-hauled passenger services in Ayrshire had been the Kilmarnock/Ayr trains, and solitary workings on Saturdays from Glasgow to Ayr during the summer of 1966, although on 3 December of that year three football specials from Glasgow to Kilmarnock were steam-hauled and on Good Friday 1967, only five weeks before the end of Scottish steam, a relief Arran boat train to Fairlie Pier was powered by Black Five no. 44699 from Glasgow's Corkerhill Depot. What was probably the last BR steam passenger working in former Sou'West territory took place on 25 September of that year when the LM Region Britannia Pacific no. 70024 worked forward from Carlisle to Glasgow with a return Blackpool Illuminations special, routed via Dumfries, Kilmarnock, Dalry and Paisley. BR officially finished with steam traction in August 1968.

Since then there have been several steam excursions to Ayr, Kilmarnock, and even Stranraer on one recent occasion, powered by preserved locomotives, while thanks to the Ayrshire Railway Preservation Group the sound of steam can now be heard in the hills around Dalmellington at the Scottish Industrial Railway Centre.

Hopefully, this selection of photographs covering the 1950s and '60s will bring back memories of Ayrshire's railways before they became the unreliable and fragmented system of today.

On 18 October 1955 the rebuilt Royal Scot 4-6-0 no. 46113, 'Cameronian', leaves Kilmarnock with the 9.20 a.m. 'Thames–Clyde Express' from Glasgow (St Enoch) to London (St Pancras). Other Anglo–Scottish services using the Nith Valley route during this period were the 4.00 p.m. from St Enoch to Leeds, the 5.30 p.m. to Penzance from St Enoch, the 9.05 p.m. sleeping car train to St Pancras from St Enoch, and the 10.25 p.m. sleeper from Glasgow Central to London Euston.

One of the more bizarre examples of the nineteenth century railway rivalry was the Caledonian's Lanarkshire & Ayrshire line which, as completed from Newton and Cathcart to Ardrossan (with branches to Kilbirnie and Irvine), duplicated existing G&SW facilities. As with other instances of this situation, the interloper was first to close and the local passenger service beyond Uplawmoor ended in 1932. However, a former link between the two routes at Lugton was retained until the mid-1960s and in this photograph the link is seen being traversed by Black Five no. 45010 with one of six specials returning from King's Park Station to Kilmarnock, Darvel and New Cumnock following the Rangers v Kilmarnock cup final at Hampden Park on 23 April 1960.

The rebuilt Royal Scot no. 46117, 'Welsh Guardsman', leaves Kilmarnock on the final leg of its 228½ mile journey with the 10.35 a.m. from Leeds to Glasgow (St Enoch) on 29 January 1955.

Kilmarnock Station in the declining days of steam, with the Jubilee 4-6-0 no. 45660, 'Rooke', taking water before continuing to Glasgow (St Enoch) with the Saturday 0930 from London (St Pancras) on 7 August 1965 (the twenty-four hour clock was introduced to timetables that summer). For the local Grozet Fair the diesel-worked service to Ayr had been replaced by steam-hauled trains of greater capacity and the standard class 4MT 2-6-0, no. 76098, is seen on the other side of the platform with the 1925 departure.

'A great big black brute of a locomotive with lots of wheels' was how one journalist described the class 9F 2-10-0, no. 92023, which was one of the class experimentally fitted with a Franco-Crosti type of boiler intended to increase efficiency by re-using hot exhaust gases. It was running trials between Carlisle and Kilmarnock when photographed being turned at Hurlford Motive Power Depot on 18 October 1955. The 'Crostis' ultimately did not produce any significant improvement in efficiency and because of corrosion problems, to say nothing of the unpleasant working conditions they caused on the footplate, engines fitted with them were converted back to normal working a few years later.

The locomotive shed at Hurlford, two miles south of Kilmarnock, had been opened by the G&SW in 1876 and was closed by BR in 1966. This typical line-up was taken on an April evening in 1963 and shows the former Caledonian 0-6-0 no. 57572, the LMS 2-6-0 no. 42879, and Black Five no. 45007.

Mauchline, closed in 1965, was the junction station for the line to Ayr via Annbank. Photographed on 27 August 1955, Black Five no. 45480 stands at the branch platform with the 11.20 a.m. Saturday train from Dumfries to Ayr. The ugly concrete lamp standards, completely out of keeping with the station buildings, were installed by BR.

Ballochmyle Viaduct, with a Black Five crossing with an up freight, photographed on 15 September 1962. This was a rather hurried shot as the field from which it was taken was occupied by a large bull! When the viaduct was completed in 1850 its central arch, with a span of 181 feet and a rail level of 163 feet above the River Ayr, was the largest stone arch in the world.

Black Five no. 44977 passes Auchinleck with a southbound mixed freight, typical of the steam era, on 15 September 1962. The station was closed in 1965 but reopened in 1984.

Steam locomotives consumed large quantities of water – a Black Five's tank carried 4,000 gallons which would last for only some fifty or sixty miles – and water troughs were installed on some main lines to obviate delays caused by taking water at stations. The tender tank was refilled by means of a scoop activated from the footplate as the locomotive passed over the troughs which, in Ayrshire, were installed by the LMS on a level stretch of track at Upper Cairn, north of New Cumnock. This photograph, taken on 26 October 1963, shows Black Five no. 45066, with a down freight, taking water at that location.

The Ayrshire coalfield saw the widespread use of industrial pugs, many of which came from the Kilmarnock works of Andrew Barclay, Sons & Co. Ltd, founded in 1840. Several of these pugs outlived main line steam. On 12 April 1968 this NCB Scottish South Area 0-4-0 saddle tank, no. 15, built by Barclay in 1924, was to be seen on the Bank Colliery branch at New Cumnock where it was employed tipping sludge from the washer at Knockshinnoch Castle Colliery. Bank Colliery closed in May 1969 and the engine was reported to have been scrapped where it stood.

Black Five no. 44795 runs into New Cumnock Station with the 12.00 noon semi-fast service from Glasgow (St Enoch) to Carlisle on 27 July 1963. This station was closed in 1965 but reopened twenty-six years later.

On 27 July 1963 Jubilee no. 45580, 'Burma', was in charge of an 8.45 a.m. additional train from Blackpool to Glasgow (St Enoch) and was photographed going well near Kirkconnel. It was one of six specials using the Nith Valley route that afternoon, the end of the Glasgow Fair fortnight. In contrast, the adjacent A76 road appears devoid of traffic.

Moving now from the Nith Valley to the Garnock Valley, this photograph shows a class 2P 4-4-0, no. 40579, passing through Glengarnock Station in the down direction with a train of tank wagons on 2 March 1957. The station nameboards read Glengarnock for Kilbirnie, the latter name being that officially carried until 1905 when Kilbirnie received a station of its own on the Lochwinnoch loop. This was closed in 1966.

The North Johnstone line, as the Lochwinnoch loop was officially known, was opened from Elderslie and ran along the west side of Castle Semple loch to relieve congestion on the main route on the other side of the loch and rejoined the latter at Brownhill Junction, north of Dalry, by means of a flying junction. A standard class 5MT 4-6-0, no. 73100, is seen passing beneath this on 18 May 1963 with an eleven coach special returning from Girvan to Glasgow (St Enoch).

From Brownhill Junction to Dalry there were four tracks, each neatly maintained in contrast to the slovenly standards of today, and this standard 2-6-4T, no. 80053, is seen on this stretch with the 6.05 p.m. from Kilmarnock to St Enoch on 18 May 1963.

Prior to electrification in the 1980s, Dalry Station had a pair of island platforms and on the rain swept evening of Glasgow Fair Monday, 15 July 1963, Black Five no. 45463 calls with the 6.25 p.m. from St Enoch to Kilmarnock.

In the great freeze of 1962–63 this standard class 4MT Mogul, no. 76001, passes the former Montgreenan Station (opened in 1878 and closed in 1955) with the 1.15 p.m. from St Enoch to Kilmarnock via Dalry on 9 February 1963. Although the local service ended three years later the line was retained until 1973.

A class B1 4-6-0, no. 61261, passing Kilwinning Junction, where the Ayr and Largs routes part company, and heading the summer Saturday 3.05 p.m. from Edinburgh (Princes Street) to Ayr on 17 August 1963. Although of LNER (rather than LMS) design, no. 61261 proved a popular engine at Ayr shed and was often to be seen on special workings.

Kilwinning Station, photographed on 29 June 1955, with the 2-6-4T, no. 42190, at the platform with the 7.45 p.m. train from Girvan to Glasgow. The Largs line is on the right.

During the latter half of the nineteenth century the G&SW and Caledonian Railways were in competition for the Arran via Ardrossan traffic and when the Caley completed a route of its own to Montgomerie Pier (while the Sou'West continued to use Winton Pier) the journey time from Glasgow to Brodick was cut to ninety minutes which compares very favourably with today's lethargic two hours or more. However, by the end of the Second World War much of the Caledonian line had become disused and, so as to serve Montgomerie Pier with its Irish and Isle of Man traffic, a connection was inserted at Stevenston where the routes crossed. The photograph shows Black Five no. 45499 using this connection to reach the former Stevenston Moor Park Station with an Orange Walk special on 5 July 1958.

Jubilee no. 45658, 'Keyes', leaves Saltcoats with a ten coach 12.25 p.m. St Enoch to Largs relief train on Glasgow Fair Monday, 20 July 1964. There were no less than fourteen specials to Largs that day, although not all were steam worked, and this locomotive from Leeds (Holbeck) Motive Power Depot had been commandeered to work to the coast.

The Queen's Birthday Holiday in 1966 fell on Monday 30 May, a sunny and warm day. Day trippers are seen here leaving one of several steam hauled relief trains from St Enoch at Ardrossan's South Beach Station, watched by the footplate crew of the standard class 2-6-4T, no. 80051. Both driver and fireman have eschewed their grease top caps for the knotted handkerchief which was *de rigueur* for BR firemen in such weather. Less than a year later the Scottish Region had finished with steam traction.

Black Five no. 45119 passing through the former Caledonian Station at Ardrossan (North), by then closed by the LMS, on 18 August 1959. It was pulling a special train returning to Newcastle from Montgomerie Pier, the passengers having enjoyed a cruise to Arran.

Winton Pier, Ardrossan, the one-time rival to Montgomerie Pier, seen on the same evening as the previous photograph with a 2-6-4T, no. 42697, leaving with the 5.45 p.m. Arran boat train for Glasgow (St Enoch).

Largs made a comparatively late appearance on the railway map as it was not reached from Ardrossan until 1885. The attractive glass-roofed station, already halved in size by Beeching's axe, was reduced to a ruin by a runaway electric multiple unit in 1995 and only recently have the squalid portakabins been replaced by a structure more suitable for the town. This photograph was taken on 18 May 1961 and shows a standard class 5, no. 73079, departing with the 6.20 p.m. for Glasgow (St Enoch).

There was never an engine shed at Largs, the facilities at Ardrossan being considered sufficient, but a turntable was necessary in steam days and Black Five no. 45456 is seen using this on 18 May 1961 after working the 2.50 p.m. from Glasgow.

The ICI Nobel's explosive works at Ardeer occupied a large area of sand dunes around Stevenston with extensive siding accommodation, a branch used by workers' trains, and to the south the rather oddly named Snodgrass branch which joined the Ayr line at Bogside (Racecourse) Station. It was at this latter location that this class 3F former Caledonian Railway 0-6-0, no. 57627, was photographed hauling a train of gunpowder vans on 15 July 1963.

A useful cross-country link, opened as early as 1848 and closed in 1964, was from Crosshouse (on the Kilmarnock–Dalry line) to Irvine. On 17 July 1964 this former Caledonian Railway 0-6-0, no. 57579, was photographed near Dreghorn heading the 3.12 p.m. Ardrossan (Town) to Darvel.

The original Troon Station, later known as Troon (Old) and used as a goods depot, was replaced in 1892 by a new structure on a loop from Barassie and more convenient for the town centre. On 21 May 1956 a class 2P 4-4-0, no. 40574, calls with the 5.08 p.m. local train from Kilmarnock to Ayr.

A standard class 3MT 2-6-0, no. 77015, crosses the River Irvine near Gatehead with the 6.22 p.m. from Kilmarnock to Ayr on 25 June 1960. This bridge, dating from 1865, was the replacement of a timber bridge which was built around 1846 so that the line could avoid a sharp curve on the approach to the original Kilmarnock & Troon Railway Bridge. The remains of the latter (inset) lay a quarter of a mile upstream and has since been restored, with its four arches, each of forty feet span, reaching twenty-five feet above the water.

A standard 2-6-4T, no. 80091, arrives at Barassie on 22 June 1963 with the 3.53 p.m train from Kilmarnock and is about to join the main line for Ayr. This local service ended in 1969.

Falkland Junction Yard at Ayr was a busy place and even today continues to deal with a considerable traffic in coal. On 22 June 1963 a standard 2-6-4T, no. 80052, threaded its way through the profusion of tracks with a 6.52 p.m. relief train from Ayr to Glasgow.

Situated at the south end of Falkland Junction Yard is Newton-on-Ayr Station which opened in 1886. New buildings were authorised in the early 1950s at a cost of £11,000. At the start of what was to be a glorious summer, a well turned out Black Five, no. 45161, calls with the 10.30 a.m. from Edinburgh (Princes Street) to Heads of Ayr on 18 June 1955.

To Sou'West men the Caley was the 'auld enemy' and here at Ayr, flaunting the sky blue livery of the old rival in the very heart of Sou'West territory, is preserved Caledonian 4-2-2, no. 123, which was built in 1886 and restored to working order in 1958. It arrived on 17 May that year with an excursion from Glasgow. Its two coaches were also of Caley origin.

Caledonian locomotives were not an unfamiliar sight in former G&SW territory following the railway grouping of 1923, although they were generally relegated to freight work after the introduction of LMS standard types and later BR-built locomotives. This former Caledonian Railway 0-4-4T, no. 55240, was photographed acting as pilot at Ayr Station on 18 June 1955, but the need for this ended in 1959 when DMUs (which did not need to be shunted) took over the Glasgow service.

Super power at Ayr on 15 July 1963 in the form of the Coronation class Pacific no. 46223, 'Princess Alice', from Glasgow's Polmadie Depot. It was awaiting departure with a 5.00 p.m. return race special to St Enoch.

A class 4P compound 4-4-0, no. 41155, pilots one of the ubiquitous Black Fives, no. 45116, out of Ayr with a relief Irish boat train from Glasgow (St Enoch) to Stranraer Harbour on 3 July 1954.

The Maidens & Dunure Light Railway was opened in 1906, in effect forming a single track loop along the coast between Ayr and Girvan, but the passenger service was withdrawn as early as 1930 (except for the Girvan to Turnberry section, serving the railway hotel, which survived until 1942). Freight traffic ceased in 1955. During the Second World War there was a Royal Navy establishment at Heads of Ayr and by 1947 this had become a Butlin's holiday camp with its own station, which stood to the east of the previous station of the same name. It was served by a shuttle service from Ayr on summer Saturdays and, photographed on 18 June 1955, happy campers arrive by the 2.43 p.m. service headed by a class 2P, no. 40664.

In addition to the local service there were through trains from Glasgow, Edinburgh and Newcastle to Heads of Ayr. Photographed on 25 June 1960, the Newcastle train (8.15 a.m. departure) passes the former Greenan Castle goods siding, situated between Alloway and Heads of Ayr, hauled by class 6MT Pacific no. 72006, 'Clan Mackenzie'.

Also photographed on 25 June 1960, near Alloway, was the 10.30 a.m Edinburgh (Princes Street) to Heads of Ayr train with a B1 4-6-0, no. 61117, in charge.

'Crab' no. 42917 at Belston Junction on 21 May 1962 with the 12.15 p.m. empties from Ayr Harbour, comprising twenty wagons for Littlemill Colliery. At this bleak junction, situated on the Ayr & Cumnock line, reversal was required to reach the colliery which was near Rankinston, a village formerly connected to the Dalmellington branch.

As the number of steam locomotives declined and the pace of line closures quickened, outings by special train became increasingly popular, traversing forgotten branches with vintage motive power. Among such railtours which I organised on behalf of the Stephenson Locomotive Society, an enthusiast body established as early as 1909, was the 'Land of Burns' which took place on 9 May 1959. Carrying 150 members and friends, this started from Ayr and visited lines closed to passenger traffic in central Ayrshire. The train was hauled by a class 2P 4-4-0, no. 40574, well turned out by Ayr Motive Power Depot, and is pictured at Cronberry Junction where the Auchinleck to Muirkirk branch was joined by the Ayr & Cumnock line.

At the iron making and coal mining town of Muirkirk an end-on junction had been made with the Caledonian Railway from Lanark, but the former G&SW portion was closed to passengers in 1951. However, the Lanark section survived until 1964 and 'Caley bogie' no. 54504 is pictured at Muirkirk with the 7.12 p.m. to Lanark on a very wet 11 July 1953. This train was always well patronised by those having a Saturday night out as there was a late return service from Lanark at near to midnight.

On 11 September 1963 a class 5MT 2-6-0, no. 42803, has arrived at Waterside, on the Dalmellington branch, with empty mineral wagons from Ayr Harbour and replenishes its water supply after the stiff climb from Dalrymple Junction. These rather ungainly looking locomotives were a hybrid design dating from early LMS days and were nicknamed 'Crabs'. They were well thought of in Sou'West territory and remained active until the end of steam there.

The NCB Ayrshire Area 0-6-0T, no. 8, built by Barclay in 1953, shunts at Dunaskin Washer on the Waterside system on a bright autumn day in 1963. This system in the Doon Valley, formerly owned by the Dalmellington Iron Co., comprised two lines (each some three miles in length) from Waterside, running north to Houldsworth Colliery and south to Pennyvennie Colliery.

The Ayr & Dalmellington Railway was built at the instigation of the Houldsworth family to serve their ironworks at Waterside. Opened in 1856, it was soon acquired by the G&SW and remains in use today for coal traffic from Chalmerston opencast site, although the terminus at Dalmellington was abandoned when the passenger service was withdrawn in 1964. Seen here on 5 March 1955 is a class 2P, no. 40590, heading the 5.30 p.m. to Ayr.

Maybole Station presented a well cared for appearance during the fine summer of 1959 as Black Five no. 44795 drew to a stand at the platform on 8 August with the 2.20 p.m. from Glasgow to Girvan. Forty or so years later the tidy look has long gone together with the up line.

Bargany Colliery was situated in the Girvan Valley near Dailly and the siding which served it is seen in this August 1959 photograph with a standard class 4MT 2-6-0, no. 76096, passing at the head of the 4.15 p.m. from Glasgow to Girvan. The Caledonian-style route indicator, carried for the benefit of signalmen, is prominently displayed on the locomotive bufferbeam.

Scenery in southern Ayrshire varies from the farmland around Girvan to bleak moorland at Chirmorie summit on the county march of Wigtownshire, and Jubilee no. 45677, 'Beatty', was making a brisk climb of the 1 in 67 gradient from Barrhill Station onto the moors with a 2.10 p.m relief train from St Enoch to Stranraer on Glasgow Fair Saturday, 1962. The locomotive was obviously having no difficulties, but with the non-corridor coaches lacking any toilet facilities for this 100 mile journey the passengers may well have had some real problems!

Upon closure of Glasgow's St Enoch Station at the end of June 1966, and the consequent transfer of Ayrshire traffic to Central Station, it was decreed from on high that all special and relief trains on Glasgow Fair Monday, 18 July, were to be worked by modern diesels. However, when the Brush Type 4 diesel, no. D1850, failed at Troon with one such train, Ayr Motive Power Depot came to the rescue with one of its faithful old workhorses in the shape of 'Crab' no. 42795. It is pictured here near Monkton working the train forward to Ayr, complete with the defunct diesel locomotive.